ABOUT THE AUTHOR

Sophie Sparham is a writer from Derby. She has written commissions for BBC Radio 4, The V&A and The People's History Museum.

Sophie co-hosts the poetry night 'Word Wise' which won Best Spoken Word Night at the 2019 Saboteur Awards. She also became the first poet to perform at the metal festival Bloodstock Open Air that same year.

https://sophiesparham.co.uk/
Twitter: @SophieSparham
Instagram: sophie.sparham

Sophie Sparham

The Man Who Ate 50,000 Weetabix

VERVE
POETRY PRESS
BIRMINGHAM

PUBLISHED BY VERVE POETRY PRESS
https://vervepoetrypress.com
mail@vervepoetrypress.com

FIRST PUBLISHED APR 2021

Printed and bound in the UK
by ImprintDigital, Exeter

ISBN: 978-1-912565-54-2

*To my dad
and all the fathers
I adopted along the way.*

CONTENTS

Foreword by Helen Mort

FOREWORD

In the opening of her poem 'Long Distance Runner', Sophie Sparham tells us: 'If I was asked to make a film of my life / I'd capture every unextraordinary moment.' It's a beautiful, captivating line, characteristic of her work. But I don't believe there's anything ordinary, anything commonplace about Sophie. In fact, since reading her poetry, I've come to believe that - in the same way that there's no such thing as bad weather, just unsuitable clothing - there's no such thing as an ordinary moment, only ordinary ways of looking. Through these poems, I've learned to look at things harder, look longer, look better. Inside these pages, familiar sights and streets and sighs speak loud and - just as importantly - speak in their own accent.

I remember Sophie telling me that each poem she writes has a soundtrack, a song that accompanied its writing. In fact, you can find out what some of them were in her Music Index in the back of this book. In the short time that I've known Sophie's poems, their stanzas have become soundtracks for my daily life. I can't walk along one of Sheffield's edges without thinking of the 'skyline's tightrope' in 'My Friends'. I can't watch the evening approach without hearing spine-tingling lines from 'Sometimes, The Night...'. Madonna songs make me think of the brilliant ending of 'Like A Prayer': 'in your bedroom, my voice was holy.' Everything about Bruce Springsteen leads me to a Sophie Sparham poem. Everything. And now, I can't even remember Dennis Skinner - my MP when I was growing up in North East Derbyshire - without imagining him joyriding. Sophie's poems are earworms that get stuck in your head.

To say they are 'earworms' doesn't really do them justice though. Yes, Sophie is a superb performer of her work, attentive to sound and rhythm and yes, that shows in the music of this collection. But these pieces are just as skilful on the page as they are in the air, just as memorable, just as deft. And to say they are 'skilful' is not enough either because these poems are also kind. You'll meet a lot of characters in this book, but what sets Sophie's writing apart is that she truly lets people and places be themselves instead of using them in the service of art. People are not metaphors. They are just people, complex and confusing and amazing and strange. Sophie is a generous human being and it's no surprise that she's a compassionate writer.

I was lucky enough to be a very small part of the journey towards this book when I did some mentoring work with Sophie, my first return to work as a freelance writer after a long maternity leave. Not only was Sophie extremely patient, I also learned at least as much from her as she did from me. So, Sophie: thank you. Reader: you're in for a treat.

Helen Mort, February 2021

The Man Who Ate 50,000 Weetabix

My friends

hang from bedsheets in prison cells,
are identified by tattoos scattered over train tracks.
My friends are can-crushed,
my friends are cobble-stoned,
scraped like gum from the lines on tarmac.

My friends are beds in hospital corridors,
coffee stains in kebab houses wiped clean.
My friends are roadkill
my friends are *Stop!* signs,
potholed and steamrolled, chewed out nicotine.

My friends are reduced on top shelves of corner shops,
blood graffitied down alley walls and back streets.
My friends are sirens,
my friends are silent,
head on collisions, coned off crime scenes.

My friends are warnings on the backs of bottles,
statistics posted by the crime commissioner's team.
My friends are overgrown,
my friend are headstones,
ripped off and ripped up, shredded down clean.

My friends get high from public toilet windows,
walk the skyline's tightrope for summat to do.
My friends are tower-blocked,
my friends are stillborn,
rot under foot, flowers grown anew.

I hear my father

in the radio, telling tales from a cracked jukebox.
It's Sunday afternoon and this is my church.

He speaks only to me. My father talks in snare drums
and microphone spit, through distorted guitars,

in lyrics I sing over and over again. Sometimes
he speaks in white noise and I still dance.

I picture him sweating in a suburban band
practice basement, second hand guitar hanging

from his neck, equipment borrowed. Arms around
a woman in a 59 chevy. Standing between the tanks

that line Cypress Avenue, cigarette smoke against
the night sky. Mother says you don't need to see.

Belief is enough. But this current runs one way
and I want to drown myself in it. My father's words

are an answerphone message requesting revolution
thirty years ago. I ask him if he still believes

in the freedom of music. He tells me he'll be right
back after this commercial break.

Sometimes, the Night

I carry this city on my back
every smashed windowpane
every torn sleeping bag
every boarded-up doorway
every bar fight
every want and regret.
But sometimes, the night
and I walk home between broken glass
kicking cans over concrete
burning hand rolled fags.
Between terrace houses
that lean against one another
as they hold up the sky
between the crossfire of conversations
beneath 5 am streets lights.

The night and I make love
behind abandoned flats
where the cats sit and cradle
dead pigeons and rats
where the overflowing gutters
reflect the under observed sky.
A puddle of stars
blurred by foot and vision
lost to sunrise.

Sometimes, the night clings to my clothes
stinking of whiskey and rain
and god only knows, I want this
only they know
a moment so brief
so fleeting
morning dew
me and the darkness are just passing through.

Slipping the Clutch

Her body ripped the air
all exhaust pipe mouth
and roundabout eyes

hole punched into existence
single parent child, built
in concrete and mortar
learnt to love broken lines

heartbeat at 50mph
rev counter at 200bpm
she rode the night
again
and again

Yeh reet luv?
Yeah, I'm fine.

A father all distance
divided by time

only an inch on the ground
until a kiss from above
made body bag of broken glass

superhero splayed

the closest she came to flight

Slow Dancing with our Jack

Meet me at the jitty, wear your black trackies.
Tell the lads, this is a two-man job, Youth.
Tell them it's the slate tiles or the baccy
shipment. Need van for what we gotta move.

They'll say Del Boy's at it, always scheming,
yeah, a reet diamond geezer, that's me, Youth.
Can't do owt for nowt, can't wake for dreamin'.
You lead, I'll follow. Jack, we gotta move.

Ignore the piss and rats and broken glass,
take my hand and sway close to me, Youth.
Some side hesitation and sharp floor-craft.
Breakin' the law, the way we gotta move.

I failed school, only Latin I learnt
was tango, twist, jive, swing, strictly ballroom.
We hustle hard, take a magic left turn.
Quickstep the sirens. Jack, we gotta move.

Tell 'em we were skip divin', or dealin',
or robbin', tell the cops owt but the truth.
Yeah, they know me, I'm always out stealin',
man needs to survive. Jack, we gotta move.

Knife Angel

On these streets everyone wants to be a blade

have palms cling to them like clenched dog jaws
like the crucifix of a rosary

reflect multi-storeys   bus stops   streetlights

be as pointed as barbed wire
as cold as a padlock

pocketed where the world can't see

The Things I Can't Tell You, Rachel

The boy I teach would shank your dead son,
murder ghosts to haunt postcodes. So street
he has a pothole mouth everyone wants
to fill in. Even me.

Some boys are raised chest first. They only
know how to inhale, hold in breath, grow
down to fit into street names, bend spines
into gang signs.

This city is a memorial. We're lucky
to have a place to lay our flowers.

The tarmac is his unmarked grave.

The backwards walking man

retraces this city's steps, as though
each stride can will the leaves to rise
onto the trees and close every bud
in Darley Park. When he reverses to

the table in the window of Café Nero
and scrawls license plates into his
notebook by the DRI, he is waiting
for the rain to rise and day to fall

into the sky. He is making a bargain
with the clock. I last saw him on Ashbourne
Road, circling the lamp post like a
catherine wheel trying to return to a time

before the fire. People follow him
as though his feet can tear down the
To Let signs and re-open The Hippodrome,
as though he will replant the old

River Gardens and book Joy Division
at the Ajanta, lead friends from train
tracks and bridges, remove the plaques
that remind us to remember.

Is it in the jitty you sprint down?

The need to light the landfills
the production lines
the drug dens
blister the nose of dogs
that dare hunt the beast
scuttling inside of you
until you are bloated
splitting with life
coming out of yourself
birthing secrets

you will swallow your dawn
here, away from the open plans
and the bingo halls
the Sunday roast dinners
the country cottage
the 2.5 children
the rotas
the buy one get one free
double glazing happy hours

away from the daylight.
Clenched palms scream your name like a wanting.
Only the pavement answers.

Joyriding with Dennis Skinner

Everyone must spend some time being bad.
After 49 years, God knows you've earnt it.
Choose the car you've always wanted to steal,
let me smash the window. Outside the pubs
men grind together as regularly as teeth
in the jaw of one who is always hungry. We ride
past figures who spray their lovers against walls
like graffiti, tag the city with names they want
the night to know. Past those that vomit their
truths into drainpipes, mouths as open as goalposts
shooting for home. This isn't what I wanted
to show you. But understand, we grow differently
down here in the cracks, are always waiting
to be weeded out or burnt by daylight.
Leave our legacies on newspaper headlines.
Are far more interesting dead.
I've learnt to pray by pressing my foot down
on the accelerator and holding my breath.
I know I should spend a lifetime repenting
for my sins, flog myself daily to make up
for the people I have border-lined with tire marks
But you, my sweet, there's nothing left for you to do.
I can't see anything changing St Peter's mind
if you, a passenger of sin, were to lean back,
put your feet on the dashboard, close your eyes
and whisper, *Dear God, I'm coming.*

Tribute

"We are ghosts or we are ancestors in our children's lives."
   – Bruce Springsteen, *Springsteen on Broadway*

The blokes at the local boozer are suspicious
of the female Bruce Springsteen tribute act.
Give over love, they laugh. *You'll never be' Boss.*

She turns away, shakes her head, smiles
as her father buys a ticket. He never asked why
she sang about streets she hadn't walked,

convinced herself she understood Asbury Park,
why she cut her hair short, ripped sleeves
from flannelled shirts, making herself a man.

The vicar told her *Our Father's voice is sacred*
so she waited for sermons, filled the bars, the bedroom silence
with music, turned the stage into church, grew her body

into a eulogy knowing that if she could be reincarnated
she would choose to live as her father's whistle
every time Thunder Road came on the car radio.

Hand gripping the steering wheel, driving to parts unknown
he would conduct a symphony with his index finger
pointing towards the Derbyshire countryside.

Tonight, he taps his foot from the half empty dance floor,
pint in hand. *Yeh look nowt like him love*, the promoter says.
Good, her father smiles.

Like a Prayer

When I learnt Madonna had armpit hair
I began to distrust porn,

said if you were going to hold my head
it was because I wanted you to.

Neither of us came from families that
made romantic speeches or went to church.

Love was something discovered behind
the bins at Morrisons, came in litres

from the corner shop. Something, we were
told we weren't old enough to have.

So, when the time came, I spoke
the alphabet and hoped that God

or whoever could make up the words.
Holding your orgasm on the tip of my tongue

in your bedroom. My voice was holy.

21st Century Dulce

Bill went to war,
a figure amongst smoke
and bathrooms mirrors,
piss-stained boots
caught between flashing lights
crawling over bodies
to get another pint

shot down. Between the gun fire
of anthems, I saw him fight
punters, bouncers, staff
head to toe in camouflage,
the invisible man on a Saturday night.

Time at the bar boys! Quick!
Ecstasy heads left fumbling
but as the lights came up,
somebody was stumbling.
Crushed like a toy in a child's hand
he lashed out at me,
punching, kicking, floundering.

I knew he was only trying to swim
in a fermented sea. I watched him drowning.

My friend, if on some sleepless night
you too could see him, praying
for last orders, tripping over a position
never held, you would no longer call
him a man, but a house on fire
with no fixed abode.

A foreigner, who let his mother tongue roam.
Bill went to war and he never came home.

Down Bringing

Mum, we're not gonna fight standing over the hospital bed
of your father, laid out as a Friday night, slumped bar side.
You don't need to show me how you've inherited his gloves,
they were always tied round your neck and now he's the devil
thumbing a lift on your shoulder. Mum, I will not don my leotard
for you, nor make you villain, my signature move is silence.
Will not drop you over the bag of tinnies, which rattle like hollow
bones for bin men, will not leave my unwanted parts for others
to clean up. Mum, no. Not on Wilson Rd, where the boys on the estate
squawk like parakeets, repeating the sins of their fathers. Nor
at the corner shop with the rusted bike frame, wheels
long vanished. Or in the telephone box, reeking of piss and sex
and childhood. Not beneath the trainers hanging limp from
telephone lines
or behind the women sunbathing in the carpark. Mum, I will not birth
my fist through your window, nor break you like pool balls. There are
parts of you all over this city, remnants of what people have stolen.
Mum, you've been broken into too many times. There's nothing left
for me to take, so I turn the light on and leave you to shadowbox,
knowing that you are a cliff face, you will fall
despite the excuse of my swing.

Rise

Dad took me to my first gig
Ain't nowt, he said.

He lived like there was no music.
Like his hands worked the rhythm of sin.
He always needed to lift something
to raise them.

Once, I found an S Club 7 CD lodged in the glove compartment

Bring it all back.

Caught him gazing at my record collection
as though it were in code
as though it were a teacher
as though he could learn to raise his empty palm
when he didn't know the answer.
When nobody had asked him a question.

Moving Out

I downsized myself
to fit into your house
boxed up my body
beneath attic sheets
scrubbed socials
and cut corners
a cycle rinsed out
on repeat.

I downsized
to fit into you
shelved books
bleached inside clean
muted mouth
threw myself out
gave away parts
I didn't need.

I downsized
to fit you
folded
myself
away.
Shaved sides
sliced nights
spelt love
with the letters
O K.

Bedtime Story

You fly tipped your childhood home,
burnt school books like bodies left beneath bracken,
offered yourself to the butcher
as if you could cut the council estate out of you,
amputate it like a leg.
Tipex the birds from your mouth.

Later, in your detached house
your wife doesn't understand
why more people can't be like you and Mr Sugar.
She is unaware you are living a funeral.

Upstairs, you read to your daughter,
wonder if the Little Mermaid had an accent,
how she can bear to gaze at the sea.

Snow Drifting

Everyone has complicated pleasures
but me and my baby,   we like driving.

Wait for the snow to hold the earth still
wheels walk on frozen water,
dance,   elegantly sliding.

A Land Rover named Discovery,
        countryside blanketed
Sundays spent between sheets   bedroom extended.

        We always put this in second,
we're always light racing
                                              drive so fast, I fear upturning

You tell me:
Just roll, no braking.

Failed all your GCSEs
you prayer bent snowdrift

pushed to the side of the road

mind reversing over matter

still moving

teaching me to be gale blown,

between landscape and sky

The night doesn't always have to fall

my beautiful risk.

But now you're paused in greyscale
photographic

I'm always so anchored.

Body's burning diesel
brain can't afford it

you tell me, you're so tired.

Yet, out here, all is frozen
take me anywhere

we're not lost

we're going nowhere.

Bodies plaited

You paused the day when you said:

sometimes, it can fly.

The Dead Poets Inn

My father can't tell the difference between drag queens and clowns.
Either way, he never visits the circus.
Saturday night is spent drinking ales with the Derbyshire lads
at The Dead Poets,
sitting in drunken silences with construction workers and ex miners,
amateur boxers, chiseled with labour.

The men in our village communicate with their hands.
When a man throws a punch at the bar
my father knows that this is the sign language of tears.
He downs his pint and leaves.

He chose a pencil over a pickaxe,
an office instead of a building site.
My father never cries.

Derbyshire Chimes

8am Phil lines up the pints at a Spoons' in Derby
Dan says: "Youth, today's a big'un, my fake ID's turning forty!"

On the No 42 Vodka Jackie explains she don't drink vodka no more
wrestled the ICU Discounts security over biscuits best-before

On the A38 Garry smirks as he filters through stand still traffic
opens his visor and is struck in the eye by 'a-flying-sting-bastard!'

Katie finds an egg with googly eyes after a conference call
finds it isn't rubber, after throwing it at magnolia walls

Eva questions Highlander's plot at Five Lamps' telly club
Sam argues the politics of Lion King 2; racism, comedy and love

In a craft bar in town, James explains how his mountaineering course
    has gone
Simon retorts "Mate, ain't The Urals sumat that yer piss on?"

A Judas Priest tribute play to two dogs and their mum
Mr Singh shuts his window, muttering, *I've ordered those electric drums.*

At the Star Trek party the living room is a UV space disco
In the kitchen the Klingons debate The Communist Manifesto

Outside the pub, the bouncer and drag queen argue about the election
graffiti on the toilet doors reads If yer not pissed yer pregnant.

The Cod Father's neon afterglow shines down on broken stones
Amy posts her polystyrene takeaway through a letterbox as she
    stumbles home.

Grown-ups?

After Kid *by Simon Armitage*

Next customer, can I take yer order?
I see yer grew up, while me time wandered
To beer garden bockers flippin' burgers,
Shadowboxin' night in lights-out corner
Blamin' it on me mother and father
Blackin' out grief, took the cape to cover
Holes yer filled when yer became me brother.
Naw, yer wouldn't catch me in the caper
Rerunning envy towards you and 'er
Livin' crime-free, two kids and a motor.
While 'eadlines read: *Batman breakdown shocker!*
Batman lucked out! Lost red and green clover.
No longer people's saviour, no longer
Able ter shake a black dog off shoulder
Wipin' tables and takeaway numbers
Rescuing staff from rogue queue jumpers
Still a kid, none the wiser, just older.
The real joker. A motionless picture,
Sold out and dressed up. Bang! Pow! Grown over!
From quick-silver to greasy spoon cooker,
A fumble with accounts in the larder
Clingin' to a closin' sign all winter
You enjoy yer happy meal? I wonder...

Ring of Fire

When forced to sing karaoke in a Berlin bar
my brother chose Johnny Cash
mimicking the dulcet tones of my grandad.
I watched him smile, the half grin he wore
the night of his boxing match, walking the line
between the tables to the same anthem
gloves in the air
hands never truly able to grip the sky.

No-one forced him to box
yet he trained daily
treadmilling his body into valleys.
He ran between construction sites and gyms
always wearing some kind of uniform
lifting weight my father had lifted before him
bench pressing the bar from his chest.

The match was called in thirty seconds –
a nose bleed from his opponent.

My brother lost on points.

I'll do better next time, Youth, he told me
eyes focused on the ropes
as though he wanted to leave
but knew that flames licked the sides.

You wanna know where I'm from, Youth?

A line of men who grunted themselves into existence.

A Father who re-entered mother's womb
and chipped away from the inside.

A man lowered into darkness
and rebirthed in night.

A land where men let the puss of ulcers thicken on their
tongues
and set their mouths

rot themselves from the inside out.

Hack away

and hack away

Father, hollowed her out like a shell,

she collapsed on them both.

Gotta make a living, he'd say.
And I'll do owt.

The Dirtiest Windows
in Northampton

The day Edward Blake died was the same day
Alan Moore decided to be a window cleaner.
Unable to contain his passion for float glass
Alan recited windows names like a Gregorian chant
trundling through The Burrows
bucket and sponge in hand.

Awning, bay, casement, picture, jalousie.

Turning down bonuses and extensive sums
he worked by moonlight and kept irregular hours
avoided any house who's hedges seemed too pristine
or had an abundance of garden ornaments.

French, pivot, cross, transom, side light.

Alan took pride in his work
peered into the brick fish tanks
in the hope that they would peer back
that the lesbian goddess
the alien fish man
the masked terrorist
would throw open their curtains
and ejaculate themselves onto the concrete
make love to the pavements, black bins
and double yellow lines.

Awning, bay, casement, picture, jalousie.

When Alan honed his craft
he found that he was able to expand frames
stretch UPVC like elastic
create glass portals into a city double glazed with stories
that looked onto stories, that looked onto stories
views that needed to be maintained
worlds matryoshka-ed within streets names.

French, pivot, cross, transom, side light.

Survival is Insufficient

You pause when you see it,
the Star Trek emblem tattooed
in black and white on her wrist.
Would you like a bag? she asks
as you fumble with your card
at the Asda checkout.

It must be her, the same woman
who last weekend won the costume contest
for dressing as 7 of 9 at the convention,
the same woman who afterwards
told you it'd taken her the entire day
to thread that emblem to her silver catsuit.

How her colleagues laughed
when she'd asked for shift swaps.
How they'd mocked a life so alien
to Friday night drinking sessions
and days at the football.

Behind this counter, you watch her
attempt survival between the singular
chocolate bars and stack of green baskets,
remember how she paraded across
the stage holding her phaser to the ceiling
as if it were possible to shoot down the galaxy.

After School Club

Emma demands we make snowflakes in September,
draws around the lid of a peanut butter jar.
Bradley leaves his paper in the shape of a rectangle,
tells me it's the home of The Grinch.
I watch as they cut triangles,
find diamonds,
show them how things with parts missing can be beautiful.

That weekend I mistake autumn for spring,
turn green,
take a razor to my thighs and cut away parts
I no longer want
until I can rehang the mirror,
until light shines through me,
until I have melted away.

Assembly Line

The factory line murdered my father,
at least that's what my mother told us
the day he returned all unscrewed
and coming apart, flooded and rusted
from the inside.

His company spent all day making men
who test piloted living, mimicking protypes
before them until they came home
broken, and their lovers spent nights
gluing them back together.

I told my brothers that I didn't believe
it, that our father wasn't dead. He'd merely
been shrunken and swallowed by another man.
This impostor would not read bedtime stories

or search for frogs in the garden pond.
Nor did he dance whilst he pegged washing
on the line. Instead, he cursed at the birds and
stared at the paper for hours, as if on standby.

I told my brothers all we'd have to do
was wait, until he opened his mouth
long enough to sing or laugh or wail
so that our dad could climb out of him
and yell, Surprise! Did you miss me?

For now I picture our father making
a campfire in the impostor's belly.
Every night he looks up, waiting for
the ceiling to crack, waiting to catch
a glimpse of the stars.

The best song in the world

is 'Come on Eileen' by Dexys Midnight Runners.
It's true. You told me in a backstreet London pub.
The only karaoke session
where your mouth caught fire
and you threw yourself across the stage,
every dance movement, self-immolation
every out of tune note, a protest,
a deed of living.

You, who sped up and slowed down songs
just to see if you liked them better.
You, who sung in different voices
depending on mood.

I still see you, mic in hand
screaming the lyrics over and over
every time I stare at a blank page in my notebook,
wait outside an office door,
press *send*.

As if you're telling me that tonight
the stage is mine,
as if you're screaming
Come on Eileen
Come on!

Jay

I knew you were gay when you fucked me
gave me my virginity back
the first man that gifted me the right to choose
our friend's parents living room
Looney Tunes on repeat in the background.

What would your father think?
I remember the five marks
tattooed on his hand,
your face when he told you they meant:
Find em, feel em, fundle em, fuck em, forget em.

Remember, the crater he left in your skull
when you took down every BNP sign
around Ripley on your paper round,
brought them home like a cat,
jaws caressing a dead bird.

Remember the way you cried on the hill to me.
Confessed your love for him over a bottle
of Frosty Jacks and I repeated
It doesn't matter
It doesn't fucking matter
until my lips were dry and cracked.

I never told you how I carried your tears in my palms,
raised them high through street protests,
took them to church, never quite praying,
cupped them on my chest when I slept.

Years later I gifted them to the river
before we lay side by side in your bed,
you in a sleeping bag
me under covers
untouched as the sunrise.

Wrestling with Baby Jesus

Jesus tag teams five pints of Stella,
picks up a packet of salted nuts
and crushes them in his palm.
Darren yanks a wise man
from the nativity display,
throws it at Jesus's head.
This is a surprise grudge match,
winner leaves with nothing.

Jesus snaps a pool queue over his thigh,
smashes Mrs Hill's vase into pieces
over the Axminster carpet.
Darren's fist yawns into him.
Blood pours from his mouth,
his teeth, a factory line of overtime,
his eyes, broken bottles.

The dartboard sheds its numbers,
the slot machine pisses pound coins,
the man painted on the gents' door runs
into the ladies. On the telly
Wizard stop playing and place bets
from the summit of Roy Wood's beard.
An audience member at the bar rocks
on her stool burbling the Lord's Prayer:
Our father, who shart in West End
Carol now be in Spain...

The bell rings. The bartender calls time.
The landlord phones the police
and the streets fill with the birdsong of sirens.
The sky throws up a burning bowling ball,
dispersing the crowd like skittles
Come on! Jesus cries, screaming at the
torn black binbags, the footprints
of dog shit smeared across the pavement,
the graffitied *Neighbourhood Watch* sign
I'll take on all of yer! It's my birthday
and I'm celebrating.

The Man Who Ate 50,000 Weetabix

sounds like a children's story, instead of a fragment of you.
A ritual repeated at dawn, where three cardboard dormice
are sandwiched into a white bowl and eaten over seven decades.

My favourite ceremony, in which you wear suits, jeans, trackies,
drink strong tea from a chipped blue mug and read the paper,
eye up the flaws of the world. You tell me to behave, I tell you

we have no control over how we are remembered, nor what parts
of us remain. Your name is always surrounded by office chairs and
red ties, bar stools and bench presses. Areas you do not permit

me to tread. And that's fine, I keep my parts of you in the rusted
tool drawer, the silver St Christopher pendant hanging
in the bathroom, the pieces of chalk wrapped in blue cloth.

I don't care for achievements the world expects. As long as the car
has an engine and a place to go, I will climb inside. So when someone
says: *your father, your father, your father* as though reading out the

latest stocks and shares, I reply, *Yes, but have you heard how his
jaw clicks?*

Glasgow Kiss

Runaway Scotsman draped in Rolls Royce
clubbin' und boozin' und out with the boys
saw yer 'cross room, through the sweat and red mist
before you knocked me out with that Glasgow kiss

you took my hand, led me by' scruff of the neck
bought me a drink and tipped it over me head
smashed bottle on' bar, downed the last of my crisps
before you knocked me out with that Glasgow kiss

well you swung all ways as long as yer were on top
I gave yer a statement, yer gave me a number and mugshot
we got on like a house with a coal fire never lit
when you knocked me out with that Glasgow kiss.

Run Out

The day the earth closed down, they boarded up the playing
fields, the local chippy, the gyms and the tattoo parlour
where we came to confess our sins to our skin. Ordered
the beach to tell the tide to wait, angered the flowers
until they refused to bloom. Marched to your front door
and nailed a No Entry signed between your teeth. You watched
your neighbours like TV and sobbed when your favourite
characters turned against one another, screamed insults
behind curtains every time one of them stepped onto the
pavement and made you long for the start of the series,
before the character development and the grief.
In the mornings, you listened for the sound of birds
until they taped over the dawn chorus and plastered
silence down the alleyways, buried workers like coffins
and prayed over them. The news never listened to your
suggestions so you stopped trying to speak to the radio
and sang along to number one hits that came out years
before you were born. When you could no longer hold
this year in your chest, you ran like a stolen car, ignoring
the piles of fly-tipped bodies, the spread legs of supermarket
doors, the cries of traffic lights, begging to be useful.
You defied the one-way street and sprinted back to a time
when rainbows were still miracles and not frowns
in windows. Back before future was an option ticked
by a government official. Back, back in the hope of finding
a house as untouched as a photograph taken in 1993.
To a time before the postman was a flightless bird
that you gazed longingly at and wondered if others understood
that this was not the definition of freedom.

The Tip

Host a funeral for the lampshade, fern cuttings
and broken wardrobe. I wonder where the men
in orange uniforms will burn their bodies.
The man with the Captain America tattoo pours
piles of Zoo into the skip next to mine. Fills the container
with half naked women. Pray for them too.

In the van, my father shakes his fist at the
driver in front. Teaches me how to puncture sky.
The lines on the road are thin as we ride past
the scrap metal lads screaming eulogies at the
dawn chorus. Maybe they can reincarnate
the bike skeleton on the front lawn.

And the fourth wise man

was mocked by the other three
for arriving late to the birth.
A mute bard, his guitar camel-humped
his back as he walked the desert,
feet out of time.

His gift, a songbook,
every page blank. Christ knew why
the kings laughed at a body
never created. But one day, at the
precinct, I saw it;

music lodged between builders
and shopping bags, stuffed down
the seats of cars and carried out
to the dales, growing on the Hawthorne
and climbing the crags.

Music caught in the cry of crows
and cursing of men who sat
and smoked outside
the ale houses. Stung into whiskey
and sweating between chip shop paper.

Fleeing as children tried to fish it
out streams, pick it
from bushes. And every morning
when the earth turned orange
the symphony began.

Paddy Maguire Volunteers for the Chatsworth Refugee Centre

At first, he offers to take out the bins
and your hands shake as you pass him the key.
You don't look him in the eye, pretend
to file paperwork as he slings the black bags
over his back.

He tells you he noticed a kitchen vacancy and cracks
in the paint, returns the next day to help prepare
the breakfast. You catch yourself staring as he butters
the toast, spreading jam like oil paint to canvas.

He never speaks of Ireland or the troubles,
keeps mouth boxing glove tight, force fed too many fists.
But you know from the way he folds the sheets
and smiles as he offers the men sugar in their tea,
that he too has walked on water to get here.

One day, when the sky screams, you weep
like a water feature and his arms embrace you
as if you are new born. So gentle are the hands that
have thumbed counterfeit notes and shaken the collars
of the indebted. So gentle.

Today he stirs leek and potato soup on a cracked hob
and nods as you pass. In your office, the news cries
in statistics and you remember the dead jellyfish
you found on the beach when you were seven. The only border
you knew was the line of the horizon. Even then,
the sea still reflected the sky.

Breathe

after Mary Oliver's Wild Geese

You do not have to repent for your sins,
pray to Jesus, Allah or the neon sign of the adult store on the A38.
You do not have to open yourself like a flower
to every ribcage that your hand brushes against
nor push your fingers to the back of your throat
to vomit out the past from the pit of your stomach.

You do not need to search for forgiveness from gravestones
meaning from opera, The Tate Modern, or any artform
that's not been made for you.
You do not need to innovate yourself,
change the electronics industry or solve homelessness,
buy running shoes or a house,
give away words you saved for another tongue,

merely put your ear to my chest and listen
to my breath against the traffic outside.

RSVP

Sometimes, I wonder if people should attend their own funerals,
bring the date forward
so they too can drink the free bar
cry at the speeches
lower themselves into the earth.
Surely, twenty-eight isn't too early to celebrate a life?

Sometimes, I wonder if you'd still make the same decision
if we told you all our favourite memories
made collages of your face by the roadside
said, isn't he such a kind hearted person,
isn't he such a talented musician,
isn't he alive?

Once the service had finished
we'd bury your empty coffin
and carry you home
singing your name like a football chant to the street signs
repeating it over and over
like a pledge
a vow

Would you still make the same decision
if I gave you all my little nicknames for you?
Collected my throw away comments in a box
for you to store under your bed

Sometimes, I wonder if you-
Instead, I gift wrap my words for the dead
and silently grieve the living.

Sunrise Over Aldi

It won't always be like this. Somewhere
boys will put down their postcodes and weep
into tracksuits, step over double yellow lines
and loiter with one another. On the south side
of the city a mother will embrace her daughter
for the first time, try on her new name and
find that it fits her lips. *Caroline*, she will say,
Caroline, Caroline, you look beautiful.
It won't always be like this. Somewhere
a seventy-year-old birdwatcher will buy a motorbike
and find that he too can fly, a black woman
will show a mixed-race girl how to tie a headwrap
and something in her heart will leap. Somewhere,
someone will utter the words; *I love you, I miss you,*
I'm sorry.
An atheist will speak Allah and smile at the taste
of honey on his tongue, the dead will climb out of
their graves and shake those standing in line
at the bank. Somewhere, you will look down at the
stars shooting across the dual carriageway and
decide to climb off the iron railings. In the shadow
of the service station, you will wait for dawn.

Long Distance Runner

If I was asked to make a film of my life
I'd capture every unextraordinary moment:

the grooves in the bark of oak trees
the intonation of old Derbyshire tongues
the view from the top of the bus.

I'd fill my motion picture with hours
of me jogging past the Derby chippies
trying to run out of myself,

zoom in on wobbling limbs and sweating features,
keep the pacing slow, the breathing heavy,
extend the b roll, the joy of being able to do nothing
but exist.

When I was a teenager I sprinted
from script to script, mimicked the
director's style, cut to the excitement
eyed up the credits.

Now, I linger in the pauses between words,
fill myself with space and silence,
wait for my breathing to return to normal.

Funeral postcard

The weather today is beautiful.
I wish you were here.

MUSIC INDEX

'I hear my father' – inspired by Van Morrison, Bruce Springsteen and Tom Petty

'Sometimes, the Night' – written to 'Something in the Night' by Bruce Springsteen and inspired by 'Come On Up To The House' by Tom Waits

'Moving Out' - written to 'Chelsea Hotel No. 2' by Leonard Cohen

'Derbyshire Chimes' – written to Lost in the Flood by Bruce Springsteen

OTHER NOTES

'The Tip' was featured in the 30th edition of the *Riggwelter Press* released in October 2020.

'Running Out' and 'Tribute' were featured in the *Issue 27*, released in early 2021.

ACKNOWLEDGEMENTS

First and foremost, thank you to you, the reader, for buying, stealing or borrowing this book. To Helen Mort, for her tireless edits and advice, you are truly magic. To Writing East Midlands for their mentorship scheme. To the Arts Council for their DYCP grant. To Stuart at Verve for believing in the work and giving it a home. To Eva, Jamie and Simon for their edits. To Emily, for the conversations and Chris for the music. To the poetry community, who lifted me. To my mum and dad, who are pictured on the front cover, in all their glory. To Gez, for putting up with me. To the friends, who are now family. To Derbyshire, the county that raised me.

ABOUT VERVE POETRY PRESS

Verve Poetry Press is a quite new and already award-winning press that focused initially on meeting a local need in Birmingham - a need for the vibrant poetry scene here in Brum to find a way to present itself to the poetry world via publication. Co-founded by Stuart Bartholomew and Amerah Saleh, it now publishes poets from all corners of the UK - poets that speak to the city's varied and energetic qualities and will contribute to its many poetic stories.

Added to this is a colourful pamphlet series, many featuring poets who have performed at our sister festival - and a poetry show series which captures the magic of longer poetry performance pieces by festival alumni such as Polarbear, Matt Abbott and Genevieve Carver.

Like the festival, we strive to think about poetry in inclusive ways and embrace the multiplicity of approaches towards this glorious art.

In 2019 the press was voted Most Innovative Publisher at the Saboteur Awards, and won the Publisher's Award for Poetry Pamphlets at the Michael Marks Awards.

www.vervepoetrypress.com
@VervePoetryPres
mail@vervepoetrypress.com